Praise for 'My Buddy's Didn't Even Know It'

MW00978659

"This is as unique as children's books get. An authentic 9/11 story that takes readers right back to that day, with a smart approach that teaches kids how to uncover stories of heroism around them. The author skillfully turned America's darkest day into a positive learning for kids."
—**New York City Educator Kaitlin Carbonaro**

"Finally, an honest, first-person account of 9/11 for kids that tugs on heart strings while managing to spark intellectual curiosity and shine a light on everyday heroes. It's a clever, authentic work of art."
— **New York City Educator Victoria Heidel**

"This authentic, heart-warming 9/11 story is a must read. I expect it will help kids to seek deeper meaning for years to come."
— **New York City Educator Anna Maria Kohlhepp**

"This is the best September 11, 2001 story for kids yet. It will help kids to reshape perceptions about the people and world around them."
— **New York City Educator Lisa DeLuca**

★★★ DISCOVERING HEROES SERIES ★★★

My Buddy's a Hero— And I Didn't Even Know It

By **Kristie Kiernan Bouryal**

Illustrated by **Gabe** and **Haruka Ostley**

Designed by James Johnson
jamesjohnson.net

ISBN 978-0-578-42159-9

This book is dedicated to my husband and my immediate family, my greatest sources of strength, courage, support and inspiration. You are my life and my loves.

Tyler, Olivia, Sophia and Thomas, you have been blessed with heroes all around you. May you always seek context and deeper meaning and may you become the best storytellers of tomorrow.

Author's Note

Dear Readers,

"My Buddy's a Hero—And I Didn't Even Know It" is the first in the *Discovering Heroes*® series of books for kids, a sequence of true stories that encourage young readers like you to find deeper meaning while emphasizing the heroism of everyday people. The series focuses on people who instinctively respond by acting and whose bravery and courageousness stand out, especially when it's needed most.

On America's darkest day, September 11, 2001, and in the days that followed, heroes swarmed the streets of New York City, Washington, D.C., Shanksville, PA and other cities across our great country. I know this, because I was fortunate enough to encounter many of these individuals in New York City and I saw firsthand the courage and bravery so many people have inside of them.

People who live by example and do what's right when no one is looking often aren't seeking attention. For that reason, their stories frequently go untold. To learn the stories of these real-life heroes, you have to go beyond the surface, ask probing questions, be an active listener and a curious learner seeking context. You'll soon find out that when you uncover the unspoken, there are often amazing, inspiring stories to be told. As you get older, this book and others in the series will help you to see beyond initial words and character limits in social media, to discover a world with broader perspective.

This series gives voice to unsung heroes, while it encourages you to seek deeper meaning and context in your life.

I strongly believe that there are heroes all around you. Do you know who they are? Do you know the details that led to their heroic actions? Do you know what questions you would ask them if you could? Today you may not be sure, but after reading this and the rest of the series, I hope you will start to inquire and learn how their stories unfold. In time, I expect you'll be able to repeat their stories again and again, while beginning to tell your own. That's my hope for you.

Now, let's start discovering heroes—the ones I write about, and the ones in your life whose stories you haven't even heard yet. I am excited for you to read about the things Tyler, Olivia and Sophia uncover. Then for you to try their approach with people in your life so you can learn amazing things about the people you know and love.

Sincerely,

Chapter 1

Tyler, Olivia and Sophia raced to the bathroom to wash their hands and get their seats at the dinner table. The rest of the family was already seated. The night's meal was on the table, but the family was more quiet than usual. Tyler sensed something was wrong. He decided to tell a joke to try to lighten the mood.

"Hey, Grandpa, what is juicy, brown and red inside?" asked Tyler with a big smile on his face. "I don't know. What?" said Grandpa. "Tonight's meat," Tyler said as he burst out laughing along with Olivia and Sophia. "Good one, Tyler," Olivia said with a giggle. "Oh, Tyler," Sophia said as she rolled her eyes and shook her head from side to side.

The rest of the family smiled.

"What time are we leaving for the firehouse tomorrow?" Tyler's mom asked Grandpa. "Probably about 6 a.m.," he said.

"Why are you going there?" asked Tyler as he began to eat his meal. "We're going to a memorial service," Grandpa said. "What's a memorial service?" asked Sophia. "It's a ceremony to honor people who lost their lives," Grandpa responded.

Everyone at the table was quiet. Then Olivia asked in a soft voice, "Did you know the people who lost their lives, Grandpa?"

"Yes, Liv, they were our friends," Grandpa said. "How did they lose their lives?" she asked with her eyes wide. "America was attacked in multiple cities on September 11, 2001. In New York City, the attack caused two of the world's biggest buildings to collapse. Thousands of people lost their lives when that happened," he said.

"Do you miss your friends, Grandpa?" Sophia asked sadly. "Very much, Soph. I miss them very much," Grandpa said.

"Why were your friends there?" asked Tyler. "They were firefighters and they went there to save people after the attack," Grandpa said.

"Did you go there to save people?" Olivia asked. "I certainly went there hoping I would save people," Grandpa replied. "I retired from the fire department a few weeks earlier, so while I wasn't officially working that day, as soon as I heard what happened I raced to get there to see if I could help," he explained.

"How did you get there? Did you drive?" Olivia asked. "No, you couldn't drive there that day. The police weren't letting cars into the area and all the bridges and tunnels leading into the city were closed. Grandma drove me to the Rescue 5 firehouse in Staten Island and along with other emergency personnel and a politician, we took the ferry boat across the water to get there," he said.

Chapter 2

Tyler, Olivia and Sophia were shocked. They were surprised this was the first time they were learning so many details they hadn't heard before.

"Grandpa, what did you see when you got there?" Tyler asked curiously. "I saw plumes of dust clouds and smoke from the fire that had taken over the buildings earlier," Grandpa explained. "I remember it was eerily quiet," he continued.

"There were no planes in the air, no helicopters overhead—it was nothing like it would have been on a normal day. There were random pieces of paper flying in the air. Caked debris was everywhere, but the streets of downtown New York City, which we also refer to as Manhattan, were desolate," he said.

"When I started to get close to the site where the buildings fell, I started to see firefighters," Grandpa shared. "Some were slumped over sitting on the street curb. Some were walking without direction. I could tell they were devastated and in shock. They had never experienced anything like this before," he said.

"What did you do next, Grandpa?" Olivia asked, looking concerned. "I saw some firefighters I knew, so I walked towards them and then I put on the fire coat, helmet and boots that I carried with me," he said.

"Why did you need to wear that?" asked Sophia. "It was a dangerous place to be in, Soph. Fires were still burning, others were smoldering and there were large piles of steel, dust, concrete and wreckage. I needed my gear on to protect me so that I could start to climb on a big mountain of ruins that we called the pile," he told her.

"That sounds like it was so dangerous, Grandpa. Why did you climb on that?" asked Olivia. "I had a lot of experience and my many years of training taught me what to do in disasters like that one, Liv.

I knew I had to start searching for people, along with my brother firefighters and other emergency personnel," he said.

"Wait Grandpa, your brother went with you?" Olivia interrupted. "No, I don't mean my real brother, Liv. I mean other firefighters, other people I worked with so closely and cared so much about, they were like my brothers. We had to see if anyone was trapped in the rubble alive, and if they were, we had to rescue them," Grandpa explained.

"We searched for hours with the smoke burning our eyes," he said. "We were climbing from one side of the pile all the way to the other side—it was an enormous amount of space," said Grandpa.

"Was anyone trapped?" asked Tyler. "Yes, Tyler, near where I was, two survivors were found alive but they were buried about 30 feet below the rubble. We made our way to them through a human chain of firefighters, police, members of the military and other emergency personnel. The two survivors were men. They were near each other but one was several feet below the other. There was a lot of debris between them, so we tried to rescue them separately," he explained.

"Now, remember," Grandpa continued, "this was a huge site of wreckage. All of the tools that we would normally be able to easily grab off of the fire truck we didn't have access to. The trucks that were there were demolished and other trucks couldn't get close to the site. The pile wasn't sturdy so heavy machines weren't near there either. We were digging with our hands and that human chain of firefighters, police and others handed debris off to each other to clear it away from the area," Grandpa told them.

Chapter 3

Sophia couldn't help but wonder what Grandpa must have felt like during that rescue. "Grandpa, were you scared?" she asked. "Soph, all I was focused on was getting that man out alive. That's all every person there was focused on," he said.

"We all worked for hours digging, moving big pieces of concrete, steel beams, trying to wedge ourselves between the debris and the man to get him free. This went on for hours," he continued. "It went on so long, that we had to work in teams to let people rest because the conditions were awful. There was heavy smoke and it was dark, wet and cold. We were shivering and nauseous from inhaling all the smoke from the fires that were still

burning."

"Did you get him out?" Olivia asked. "Ultimately, we did. Teams of people came together and worked for hours to free him from the rubble. The man that was trapped near him was also rescued, but a few hours earlier," Grandpa said.

"Did you find anyone else?" Tyler asked. "Another group of rescuers freed a woman a little while later. But we kept looking for others for days and weeks," Grandpa explained, "and he was the last man we were able to get out alive," he said.

"Wait, so you helped rescue the last man out of the ruins alive?" asked Tyler. "Yes, I helped," Grandpa replied. "You are very courageous and brave," Olivia said as Sophia and Tyler nodded in agreement.

"I want you all to remember something important," Grandpa said. "There will always be people trained for disasters who risk their lives to take care of other people," he explained. "People often help without knowing what it will take, but not knowing will never stop them from doing what's needed," Grandpa said.

"Together, people can achieve a lot more

than individually," Grandpa continued. "I saw Americans come together on September 11, 2001 and in the many days, weeks and months that followed, to help in any way they could. September 11th was America's darkest day. While it sure didn't seem it at the time, when I think back on it, goodness did prevail that day and I believe it always will," Grandpa said.

"I had no idea my buddy is a hero," Tyler said, as he smiled proudly and walked towards Grandpa with his arms open to give him a hug. "Me either," said Olivia and Sophia as they quickly joined in the group hug. "We love you, Grandpa," Tyler said as Olivia and Sophia nodded and said the same. "I love you more," Grandpa said, "I love you more."

Chapter 4

"Grandpa, can we come to the memorial tomorrow?" asked Tyler. "Yeah, I want to go too," said Olivia. "And me, too," said Sophia. "If you really want to, sure you can come," Grandpa replied.

The next morning, the family drove together to the Rescue 1 firehouse for the ceremony. The doors of the firehouse were open, and dozens of people were in front greeting each other with warm hugs and handshakes.

"Hey, John!" one man shouted with a smile on his face as he walked towards Grandpa and gave him a big, long hug. The man turned to Tyler, Olivia and Sophia and said, "Do you kids know your Grandpa is a hero?" Tyler, Olivia and Sophia

15

turned towards Grandpa and gazed at him proudly.

Now they do, because they asked good questions and through Grandpa's responses, his story of heroism started to unfold. Now Tyler, Olivia and Sophia can't wait to ask Grandpa more questions so they can learn about the friends he lost on September 11th and other heroic things he may have done.

As they looked around the firehouse full of people, their minds couldn't help but wonder about the men they were all there to remember: What would they learn about them and how many other stories of heroism are waiting to be told?

In the next book in the *Discovering Heroes*® series, Tyler, Olivia and Sophia learn about some of Grandpa's brave friends and brothers who lost their lives on September 11, 2001. Find out more at www.contextproductions.com.

Word List

'My Buddy's a Hero—And I Didn't Even Know It'

There are some words in "My Buddy's a Hero—And I Didn't Even Know It" that you may not be familiar with, so we asked Grandpa to explain what he means by them in this word list, also known as a glossary of terms, you can refer to as a reminder.

Debris
Debris is pieces of the buildings and other broken materials spread out across the large area where the buildings once stood.

Desolate

The streets were completely empty. There were no people, no moving cars, buses or taxis, no hot dog stands—all of the things you would expect to see in downtown Manhattan weren't there.

Eerily

It was odd and strange that there was no noise in Manhattan because it's usually very loud and busy.

Manhattan

Manhattan is another name for New York City.

Plumes

Plumes of smoke are giant, thick clouds of smoke rising high into the sky. They covered downtown Manhattan that day and they could be seen miles away.

Retired

I worked for more than 20 years in the Fire Department of the City of New York (FDNY). I met the department's requirements for the number of years I needed to work, plus and I reached an age that was old enough to stop working, so I did.

Rubble and Ruins
Pieces of the buildings that collapsed and everything that was in them.

Smoldering
Fires burn with flames, but when the flames go away, whatever is burning is still hot and you can see smoke coming off of it.

About Grandpa

Grandpa is a loving husband, father of four daughters and a former lieutenant in the Fire Department of the City of New York, where he valiantly served for more than two decades. For about 17 of those years, he was assigned to three of the department's five elite rescue units—Rescue 1, Rescue 2 and Rescue 5.

About Tyler, Olivia and Sophia

Tyler is an 11-year-old with an infectious spirit and smile who loves America, his family, baseball, football, fishing and being creative.

Olivia is a bright-eyed, determined, 8-year-old who loves an intellectual challenge, art, baking, softball, dance, basketball and video on demand.

Sophia is a witty, playful 6-year-old with a sheepish smile and a sly spirit who loves animals, music, cooking, swimming, gymnastics, mobile devices and video on demand.

About the Author

Kristie Kiernan Bouryal is an author and an accomplished communication and marketing strategist with more than 25 years of experience building brands, demand and revenue generation across multiple industries. She has a proven track record of success in executive roles spanning global corporate communications, marketing and all forms of media.

Kristie has received numerous awards and recognition throughout her distinguished career including an International Business Award for Brand Renovation from the Stevie® Awards; Gold Quill Excellence Awards from The International Association of Business Communicators; multiple Gold Hermes Creative Awards from the

Association of Marketing and Communication Professionals; the Chairman's Prize for Innovation at The Associated Press; and the news industry's prestigious Peabody Award.

Kristie is a graduate of Syracuse University's S. I. Newhouse School of Public Communications. She is a loving wife, sister, aunt and the oldest of four girls born to a now retired nurse and a former lieutenant in the Fire Department of the City of New York's elite rescue units. Kristie was born and raised in Staten Island, New York and currently resides in New Jersey with her husband.

About the Illustrators

Gabe Ostley was born in Minnesota and graduated from the Savannah College of Art and Design with a B.F.A. degree in Sequential Art. After working in illustration and licensed characters in New York City, he moved to Hong Kong where he was artist-in-residence for Yew Chung Education Foundation. There, his work expanded to include painting, art installation, murals and large-scale sculptures. While still in Hong Kong, his comic book work was published by DC Comics, Devil's Due, and numerous indie publishers and anthologies. Recently, he adapted Declan Greene's play "Moth" into a graphic novel for The Cincinnati Review. In 2018, with his artist wife Haruka, the two formed Gabruka House in Portland, Oregon. Their all-ages fantasy graphic novel project, Bokura, is a Portland Regional Arts & Culture Council grant winner.

Haruka Ashida Ostley is a multidisciplinary artist (painter/muralist/mosaic artist/performer) who was born in Japan but grew up living on four different continents with her family. After graduating from Savannah College of Art and Design with a B.F.A. in Painting, she moved to New York City, where she trained at the Stella Adler Studio of Acting. Later, she became an artist-in-residence in Hong Kong before moving back to the USA in 2015. Currently, she works in Portland, Oregon as a freelance artist creating murals, paintings, graphic novels and commissioned portraits.

Haruka enjoys working with people of different

backgrounds across different media around the world. When stories and energies fill her heart, she responds with her brush, color, body, and soul.

www.ru-ostley.com
www.gabrukahouse.com